HOW TO START A BUSINESS FOR BEGINNERS 2024

Turn Your Company Into a Money Machine and Earn Profit with your business

Abraham Scott

© **Abraham Scott, 2024.** All rights reserved. Except for brief quotations included in critical reviews and certain other noncommercial uses allowed by copyright law, no part of this book may be reproduced, distributed, or transmitted in any form or by any means, including photocopying, recording, or other electronic or mechanical methods, without the publisher's prior written permission.

Table of content

Introduction	**8**
Who This Book is for:	8
How to Use This Book	9
Chapter One	**12**
The Beginning	12
Chapter Two	**20**
Building Your Business	20
Chapter Three	**32**
Organise Your Finances	32
Chapter Four	**36**
Finance Your Business	36
Chapter Five	**46**
Expanding Your Business	46
Part Two	**50**
Chapter Six	**50**
Introduction to Entrepreneurship	50
Chapter Seven	**56**
Building Your Brand	56
Chapter Eight	**64**
Getting Past Obstacles	64
Chapter Nine	**71**
Staying Ahead of Industry Trends	71
Chapter Ten	**77**
Case Studies and Success Stories	77

Conclusion **86**
    Recap and Final Thoughts   86

Introduction

"Starting a Business for Beginners" is a welcome place! This book is meant to assist you on the thrilling path of becoming an entrepreneur, from creating your first concept to starting and running your own company. Whether you're thinking about starting your own business or are just considering being self-employed, this book will provide you with the information, resources, and motivation you need to make your goals come true.

Who This Book is for:

Anyone who: - Has a company concept but is unsure where to begin may find this book useful.
- → Is interested in discovering the essentials of launching and managing a business.
- → Is seeking doable guidance and strategies to develop a profitable company.

→ Requires direction on how to get past the typical obstacles that new business owners encounter.
→ You don't need any prior business expertise. This book helps you learn the fundamentals of entrepreneurship by simplifying difficult ideas into the language you can comprehend and using examples from real-world situations.

How to Use This Book

Use these pointers to make the most of this book:

→ **Go through each chapter in order:** The format of the book is designed to walk you through the process of launching a business step-by-step. Completing each chapter in its entirety will assist you in laying a strong intellectual foundation.

→ **Make Observations and Think Back**: As you read, record your questions, ideas, and thoughts in a journal or digital device. Consider how the details relate to your particular business concept.

→ **Finish the activities:** The activities and worksheets in this book are meant to assist you in putting what you've learned into practice. Spending some time on these will improve your comprehension and provide you with useful business insights.

→ **Make Use of More Options:** The reading lists and appendices offer insightful options for more education. Make use of them to learn more about subjects that are very important to your company.

→ **Check Out the Chapters as Required:** As you move through the process of starting a business, you might find yourself going back and reviewing some of the earlier chapters. Never be afraid to go back and read over areas that are particularly relevant to where you are in the process.

→ Establishing a business is a thrilling adventure full of possibilities and difficulties. You will have the knowledge and self-assurance to start your own business with this book as your guide. Now let's get going!

Chapter One

The Beginning

Defining your company idea, registering, launching, and developing your firm are just a few of the many critical factors that come with starting a business, which is one of the most thrilling and rewarding experiences you can have. But where do you start?

The public often hears about overnight successes because they make for a great headline. However, it's rarely that simple—they don't see the years of dreaming, building, and positioning before a big public launch.

For this reason, remember to focus on your business journey and don't measure your success against someone else's.

Consistency Is Key: New business owners tend to feed off their motivation initially but get frustrated when that motivation wanes. This is why it's essential to create habits and follow routines that power you through when motivation goes away.

Take the Next Step Some business owners dive in headfirst without looking and make things up as they go along. Then, there are business owners who stay stuck in analysis paralysis and never start. Perhaps you're a mixture of the two—and that's right where you need to be.

The best way to accomplish any business or personal goal is to write out every possible step it takes to achieve the goal. Then, order those steps by what needs to happen first. Some steps may take minutes while others take a long time.

The point is to always take the next step.

1. Determine Your Business Concept: Most business advice tells you to monetize what you love, but it misses two other very important elements: it needs to be profitable and something you're good at. For example, you may love music, but how viable is your business idea if you're not a great singer or songwriter? Maybe you love making soap and want to open a soap shop in your small town that already has three close by—it won't be easy to corner the market when you're creating the same product as other nearby stores.

If you don't have a firm idea of what your business will entail, ask yourself the following questions: What do you love to do? What do you hate to do? Can you think of something that would make those things easier? What are you good at? What do others come to you for advice about? If you were given ten minutes to give a five-minute speech on any topic, what would it be? What's something you've always wanted to do, but lacked resources for? These questions can lead you to an idea for your business. If you already have an idea, they might help you expand it. Once you have your idea, measure it against whether you're good at it and if it's profitable. You can take an existing product and improve upon it. You can also sell a digital product so there's little overhead.

What Kind of Business Should You Start? Before you choose the type of business to start, there are some key things to consider: What type of funding do you have? How much time do you have to invest in your business?

Do you prefer to work from home or at an office or workshop? What interests and passions do you have? Can you sell information (such as a course), rather than a product? What skills or expertise do you have? How fast do you need to scale your business?

What kind of support do you have to start your business? Are you partnering with someone else? Does the franchise model make more sense to you? Consider Popular Business Ideas Not sure what business to start?

Consider one of these popular business ideas:

- Start a Franchise
- Start a Blog
- Start an Online Store
- Start a Dropshipping Business
- Start a Cleaning Business
- Start a Bookkeeping Business
- Start a Clothing Business
- Start a Landscaping Business
- Start a Consulting Business
- Start a Photography Business
- Start a Vending Machine Business

2. Research Your Competitors and Market: Most entrepreneurs spend more time on their products than they do getting to know the competition. If you ever apply for outside funding, the potential lender or partner wants to know: what sets you (or your business idea) apart? If market analysis indicates your product or service is saturated in your area, see if you can think of a different approach. Take housekeeping, for example—rather than general cleaning services, you might specialize in homes with pets or focus on garage cleanups. Primary Research The first stage of any competition study is primary research, which entails obtaining data directly from potential customers rather than basing your conclusions on past data.

You can use questionnaires, surveys, and interviews to learn what consumers want. Surveying friends and family isn't recommended unless they're your target market. People who say they'd buy something and people who do are very different.

The last thing you want is to take so much stock in what they say, create the product, and flop when you try to sell it because all of the people who said they'd buy it don't because the product isn't something they'd buy.

Secondary Research Utilize existing sources of information, such as census data, to gather information when you do secondary research.

The current data may be studied, compiled, and analyzed in various ways that are appropriate for your needs but it may not be as detailed as primary research.

Conduct a SWOT Analysis SWOT stands for **strengths, weaknesses, opportunities, and threats.** Conducting a SWOT analysis allows you to look at the facts about how your product or idea might perform if taken to market, and it can also help you make decisions about the direction of your idea. Your business idea might have some weaknesses that you hadn't considered or there may be some opportunities to improve on a competitor's product.

Chapter Two

Building Your Business

Create your business plan.

A business plan is a dynamic document that acts as a road map for starting a new firm. This paper is easy for potential investors, financial institutions, and corporate executives to grasp and digest. Even if you plan to self-fund, a business plan may help you flesh out your concept and identify possible issues. When drafting a comprehensive business strategy, incorporate the following sections:

Executive summary: The executive summary should appear first in the business plan, although it should be prepared last. It defines the proposed new business, highlighting the company's aims and means for achieving them.

The company description explains what issues your product or service solves and why your business or concept is the best. For example, if you have a background in molecular engineering and have utilized that knowledge to develop a new sort of sports clothing, you have the necessary qualifications to design the greatest material.

Market analysis: This portion of the business plan examines how well a firm compares to its rivals. The market study should contain a target market, segmentation analysis, market size, growth rate, trends, and an assessment of the competitive landscape.

Organization and structure: Explain the sort of corporate organization you intend, the risk management measures you suggest, and who will be on the management team. What are their qualifications? Will your firm be a single-member limited liability company (LLC) or a corporation?

Mission and goals: This part should include a succinct mission statement that outlines what the company hopes to achieve and the measures necessary to get there. These objectives should be SMART (specific, measurable, actionable, realistic, and time-bound).

Products or services: This part explains how your business will run. It comprises what items you will provide to customers at the start of your firm, how they compare to existing rivals, how much your products will cost, who will be in charge of generating the products, how you will obtain resources, and how much they will cost to manufacture.

Background summary: This section of the business plan takes the longest to write. Compile and summarise any data, articles, or research papers on trends that may have an impact on your business or sector, both favorably and adversely.

Marketing strategy: The marketing plan defines the qualities of your product or service, summarises the SWOT analysis, and examines rivals. It also describes how you plan to promote your firm, how much money will be spent on marketing, and how long the campaign will run.

Financial plan: The financial plan is possibly the most important aspect of the business plan because the firm cannot function without money. Include a planned budget in your financial plan, as well as expected financial documents such as an income statement, balance sheet, and cash flow statement. Typically, five years of predicted financial statements are sufficient.

Develop an exit strategy: An exit strategy is essential for any firm seeking finance because it specifies how you will sell the company or transfer ownership if you decide to retire or pursue other opportunities. An exit strategy also assists you to maximise the value of your firm when it comes time to sell. There are several possibilities for departing a firm, and the ideal one for you depends on your objectives and circumstances.

The most commonly used escape techniques are:
- Selling the business to another party.
- Passing the company on to family members
- Liquidating corporate assets.
- Close the doors and go away.
- Develop a Scalable Business Model.

As your small business expands, it's critical to have a scalable business plan that allows you to accept more consumers without incurring more expenses. A scalable company strategy can be readily copied to service more clients while incurring minimal additional expenditures.

Some typical scalable business models are:

- Subscription-based enterprises.
- Businesses selling digital items
- Franchised businesses
- Network Marketing Businesses

- Start planning for taxes.

One of the most critical steps to take when beginning a small business is to begin arranging for taxes. Income tax, self-employment tax, sales tax, and property tax are just a few of the several sorts of taxes that you may be required to pay. Depending on the nature of your firm, you may be obliged to pay additional taxes, such as payroll or unemployment tax.

Choose Your Business Structure: When organizing your firm, you must analyze how each structure affects the amount of taxes you pay, everyday operations, and if your assets are in danger. An LLC minimizes your accountability for business debt. LLCs can be owned by one or more individuals or businesses and require a registered agent. These owners are known as members. LLCs provide liability protection for their owners. They are one of the easiest business organizations to set up. You can form a single-member LLC. You may have to file additional documents with your state regularly. LLCs cannot issue shares. You must pay yearly filing costs to your state Limited

Liability Partnership (LLP): An LLP is comparable to an LLC, except it is primarily used by licensed business professionals like attorneys and accountants. These arrangements need a partnership agreement. partners have limited culpability for the obligations and conduct of the LLP. LLPs are straightforward to create and need little paperwork. An LLP can have an unlimited number of partners. Partners are expected to actively participate in the business. LLPs cannot issue shares. All partners are individually accountable for any malpractice claims brought against the firm.

Sole proprietorship: If you want to establish your firm, you should think about becoming a single owner. For legal and tax reasons, the corporation and its owner are treated as the same entity. The business owner accepts responsibility for the business. So, if the firm fails, the owner is personally and financially liable for all business debts. Sole proprietorships are easily formed. There is no need to file any additional papers with your state. You have entire control of the business. You are individually accountable for all business debts. Fundraising for a lone proprietorship might be tough. The firm may have a limited lifespan.

Corporation: A corporation, like an LLC, minimizes personal liability for corporate obligations. A corporation may be taxed as a C corporation (C-corp) or a S corporation. Small firms that fulfill specific IRS standards can get S-corp status, which allows for pass-through taxes. Larger enterprises and startups seeking venture financing are often taxed as C-corporations. Corporations provide liability protection for their owners. The lifespan of a corporation is not restricted. A company may have an infinite number of stockholders.

Corporations are liable to multiple taxes. They're more expensive and hard to establish than other business arrangements. The stockholders may have limited liability. Before deciding on a business structure, consult with a small business accountant and potentially an attorney, as each business form has unique tax treatments that may affect your bottom line.

Register your business and obtain licenses: Following the selection of a corporate structure, several legal concerns must be addressed. The following is a useful checklist of elements to consider while setting up your business:

Choose Your Business Name: Make it memorable, but not overly challenging. To build your internet presence, use the same domain name if it is still accessible. A business name cannot be identical to another registered corporation in your state, nor can it infringe on another trademark or service mark that has already been registered with the United States Patent and Trademark Office.

Business Name vs. DBA: There are business names and false business names, such as "Doing Business As" or DBA. If you operate under a name other than your company's legal name, you may be required to register a DBA. For example, "Sam Bike WorkShop" operates as "Sam's Bikes." The official name of the company is "Sam Bike WorkShop," while the DBA is "Sam's Bikes". You might need to file a DBA with your state, county, or local government authorities.

The advantages of a DBA are:

- It can assist you create a business bank account under your company name.
- A DBA can serve as a "trade name" to market your products or services.
- A DBA may be used to get a business license.

Register your business and get an EIN: To start a corporation, LLC, or other business entity, file documents with your state's business department, often the Secretary of State. As part of the procedure, you'll need to select a registered agent to accept legal papers on your behalf. You will also need to pay a filing fee. The state will issue you a certificate that allows you to apply for licenses, a tax identification number (TIN), and commercial bank accounts.

Next, apply for an employment identification number (EIN). All firms, excluding sole proprietorships with no workers, require a federal employment identification number. When you submit your application to the IRS, you will normally get your number within minutes.

Obtain the appropriate licenses and permits: Your industry and jurisdiction will decide the legal requirements. Most companies require a combination of municipal, state, and federal licenses to operate. Check with your local government agency (or an attorney) for licensing information specific to your location.

Chapter Three

Organise Your Finances

Keep your personal and business funds apart. This article explains how to select a company checking account and the need for distinct business accounts. The business name and business tax identification number (EIN) are required when opening a business bank account.

You may use this business bank account for all of your firm's transactions, including billing clients and suppliers. A bank will often need a separate business bank account to grant a business credit line or loan.

Invest in accounting software or hire a bookkeeper to handle and maintain inventory if you sell products, your accounting software must have an inventory component. Financial statements should be able to be generated by the program, together with ledger and journal entries.

Certain software applications are also useful for bookkeeping. These frequently have functions like writing checks and handling payables and receivables. This program also allows you to create invoices, run reports, manage your revenue and spending, and compute taxes.

You may get several bookkeeping services that can handle all of this and more. These online services are accessible from any computer or mobile device and frequently come with features like invoicing and bank reconciliation. Examine the top accounting programs for small businesses or decide whether you want to do your bookkeeping.

Find the Point at Which You Break Even: You need to determine your beginning costs before you can secure funding for your company. Make a list of everything you need in terms of physical materials, figure out how much professional services will cost, find out how much it will cost for any licenses or permissions you need to function, and figure out how much office space or other real estate would cost. Include the payroll and benefit costs, if they apply.

It's preferable to overestimate the initial costs and have too much money than not enough, as businesses might take years to earn a profit. Having enough cash on hand to cover six months' worth of operational expenditures is advised by several experts.

You must ascertain the point at which your firm turns a profit once you have determined how much you need to launch it. This is the amount at which you break even.

The break-even point is equal to the contribution margin ÷ fixed cost. However, the contribution margin is calculated as follows: total sales revenue - product manufacturing cost.

Chapter Four

Finance Your Business

There are several options for financing your company; some are more straightforward to get, while others demand a significant amount of work. There are two types of funding: external and internal.

Within-funding comprises; Individual savings Credit histories, Money received from relatives and friends.

If you use credit cards or your own money to finance the firm, you will be responsible for paying off the debt on the cards and will lose some of your wealth if the business fails.

You run the danger of strained relationships and bitter sentiments if you let your family or friends invest in your business if it fails. Owners of businesses that wish to reduce these risks should think about obtaining outside finance.

Among the outside financing sources are: loans for small businesses, grants for small businesses Angel financiers, Venture capital Using crowdsourcing. Small companies could need to combine funding from several sources.

Take into account the required amount of money, the time it will take the firm to return it, and your level of risk tolerance. Whichever supplier you choose, make a profit in mind. Getting paid six figures is significantly better than making seven figures and keeping just $80,000 of that money.

Ideas for funding include: **Factoring invoices:** You may sell your outstanding bills to a third party for a profit by using invoice factoring.

Credit lines for businesses: Apply for a company credit line; these are comparable to personal credit lines. The income, credit score, and financial history of your company will determine the credit limit and interest rate.

Financing for equipment: You may use a loan or lease to pay for pricey equipment that you need to buy for your company.

Microloans from the Small Business Administration (SBA): Microloans, which have a maximum loan amount of $50,000, can be utilized for equipment or machinery, working capital, inventory, or supplies.

Funds: Businesses that support innovation, export expansion, or are based in historically underserved areas are eligible to apply for funds from the federal government. Grants are also available from regional and local organizations.

crowdsourcing: By asking for donations or selling stock in your business, you may use crowdsourcing to raise money from a sizable number of individuals.

Take into account your risk tolerance, the length of time you have to repay the loan, and the amount of money you need for your business when selecting the best funding source.

Make a Business Insurance Application: Even if your company is a home-based venture or you don't hire anyone, you still need insurance. Your company strategy and the dangers you encounter will determine what kind of insurance you require. You may require more than one kind of policy, and if your company expands, you may require more coverage. If you have employees, you are legally obligated to have workers' compensation insurance in most states.

To Obtain Insurance, Consult an Agent: An insurance professional may assist in identifying the right coverages for your company and locating plans from the most affordable insurers. An independent insurance agent may compare rates and coverage alternatives from many insurers since they represent a number of them.

Your company is shielded from third-party claims of property damage, personal injury, and physical harm, including defamation and false advertising, by liability insurance. Your company's tangible assets, such as your inventory, equipment, and office space, are covered by property insurance.

If your company has to temporarily close because of a covered event, such as a natural disaster, business interruption insurance can reimburse you for your lost revenue. Insurance covering product liability guards against allegations that your goods caused property damage or physical harm.

Claims from workers alleging sexual harassment, discrimination, or other wrongful terminations are covered by employee practices liability insurance. When an employee is hurt at work, workers' compensation insurance pays for their medical bills as well as their lost income.

Obtain the Appropriate Business Equipment

Your life may be easier and your firm can function more efficiently with the use of business tools. You can automate chores, save time, and improve decision-making with the correct tools using Accounting software, Keeping tabs on your company's earnings and outlays, financial reports, and submitting tax returns.

Promote Your Company: Many entrepreneurs spend so much money developing their goods that, by the time they launch, they have little money left over for marketing. Or maybe they've been working on the product for so long that marketing is a secondary concern.

Establish a Website: Having a website is crucial, even if your business is physical. In addition, building a website is a quick process that can be finished in a weekend. You may create an e-commerce website to sell goods online, or you can create a conventional informative website. Provide a page on your website with your locations and business hours if you sell goods or services offline. It is recommended to include other pages such as an "About Us" section, product or service pages, FAQs, a blog, and contact details.

Make Your Website SEO-Friendly: Once you have an online business or website, concentrate on search engine optimization (SEO). In this manner, the search engine might direct a prospective buyer to your website when they type in particular terms related to your goods. Even if you're utilizing all the proper keywords, SEO is a long-term plan, so don't anticipate a tonne of traffic from search engines straight away.

Produce Relevant Content: Make it simple for visitors to your website to locate the accurate answers to their inquiries by offering high-quality digital information. Ideas for content marketing include blog entries, demos, videos, and client endorsements. Think of content marketing as one of the most important things you should do each day. Posting on social media is combined with this.

Obtain Listings in Internet Directories: Consumers search for local companies using Internet directories such as Yelp, Google My Business, and Facebook. Business directories are also available at several chambers of commerce and city halls. Add your company to as many directories that are pertinent to it as you can. Additionally, you may add entries for your company to industry-specific directories.

Create a Plan for Social Media: You should be present on social media as your potential clients use it daily. Share engaging and pertinent material with your audience. Utilize social media to direct visitors back to your website, where they can purchase your goods and services and find out more about you.

It's not necessary to use every social media network that exists. But since Facebook and Instagram include e-commerce capabilities that let you sell straight from your social media profiles, you should be active on these platforms. Free ad training is available on each of these platforms to assist you in marketing your company.

Chapter Five

Expanding Your Business

You must increase both your clientele and income to develop your company. This may be achieved by increasing the scope of your marketing initiatives, refining your current offering, working with other creators, or introducing new goods or services that enhance your current portfolio.

To free up time to concentrate on growing the firm, consider automating or outsourcing some jobs. For instance, if social media marketing is consuming too much of your time, think about managing your accounts more effectively with a tool like Hootsuite. Another option is to fully outsource the time-consuming task.

Technology may also be used to automate some corporate functions, such as lead generation, email marketing, and bookkeeping. You'll have more time if you do this to concentrate on other facets of your company.

Ensuring you're financially successful while growing your company requires close attention to your finances. You must either discover strategies to raise your revenue or cut expenses if your income is insufficient to pay your bills.

Form a Group: As your company expands, you'll need to assign responsibilities and assemble a group of individuals to assist you in managing the day-to-day operations. This might entail bringing on more employees, independent contractors, or freelancers.

Resources for forming a group consist of:

- **Recruiting platforms:** You may publish job descriptions, check resumes, and conduct video interviews with prospects using recruiting services like Indeed and Glassdoor to locate the perfect ones.

- **Job boards:** You may post available positions on job boards like Indeed and Craigslist for free.

- **Social media:** To locate possible workers, you may also use social media sites like Facebook and LinkedIn.

- **Platforms for freelancers:** You may locate skilled independent contractors for one-time or temporary assignments by using Upwork, Freelancer, and Fiverr. Certain responsibilities, including bookkeeping, social media marketing, and customer support, can also be outsourced.

Another option is to think about collaborating with companies in your sector. If you're a wedding planner, for instance, you may collaborate with a caterer, venue, photographer, or florist. By doing this, you can provide your clients with a one-stop shop for all of their wedding requirements.

An online retailer that collaborates with a fulfillment center is another illustration. This kind of collaboration can help you deliver your goods to clients more quickly and save money on storage and shipping.

Look for companies that fit your niche in your sector to form possible alliances. For instance, as a web designer, you may collaborate with a company that specializes in digital marketing.

Additionally, you might look for companies that provide distinct goods or services to your target client but serve the same market. If you offer men's or women's clothes, for instance, you may collaborate with a jewelry retailer or a hair salon.

Part Two

Chapter Six

Introduction to Entrepreneurship

Entrepreneurship is the process of starting, growing, and managing a new company to make money, innovate, or meet market demand is known as entrepreneurship. To bring a business concept to reality, one must recognize possibilities, take measured risks, and overcome barriers. Because they spur economic development, create jobs, and stimulate innovation, entrepreneurs are vital to the economy.

The following are important facets of entrepreneurship:

- **Innovation:** Creating new goods, services, or methods that provide clients with special benefits.
- **Risk-taking:** Making time, financial, and physical investments in a project that could not succeed.
- **Opportunity Recognition:** Finding market holes and creating fixes.
- **Resource Management:** Making effective use of resources, including money, people, and technology, to meet organizational objectives.

Characteristics of Profitable Entrepreneurs

The traits that successful business owners frequently possess help them overcome the difficulties involved in launching and maintaining a company. Among these characteristics are:

1. Passion: A strong desire to see their company concept succeed and a great deal of excitement for it.

2. Resilience: The capacity to overcome obstacles and carry on in the face of setbacks.

3. Creativity: An inventive way of thinking that lets people come up with original ideas and solutions.

4. Vision: A long-term view of how to accomplish their objectives and a clear grasp of what they are trying to achieve.

5. Adaptability: The ability to change course and modify plans in response to evolving facts and market dynamics.

6. Risk Tolerance: Consistency in taking measured chances and making choices in the face of uncertainty.

7. Strong Work Ethic: A commitment to investing the time and energy required to expand the company.

8. Leadership: The capacity to forge a cohesive team, encourage and inspire others, and provide a favorable work environment.

9. Financial Acumen: Knowledge of budgeting, investing, and financial management.

10. Networking Skills: The capacity to form bonds with others and make use of connections to get chances and assistance.

Although launching a business has many benefits, there are drawbacks as well. Being aware of the advantages as well as the challenges will help you get ready for your entrepreneurial endeavors.

Financial Potential: Possibility of generating large sums of money and becoming wealthy.

Creative Freedom: The capacity to invent and realize your concepts.

Personal Growth: The opportunity to learn new abilities, get over obstacles, and realize one's potential.

Impact: Possibility of boosting the economy, generating employment, and improving your neighborhood or sector.

Difficulties: -Credit Risk: The potential for investment loss or unstable finances.

Time Commitment: The substantial time and work needed to launch and expand a business.

Uncertainty: The necessity of navigating unknowns and the absence of success assurance.

Pressure and Stress: Managing a business may put a person under pressure and cause burnout.

You bear the responsibility for the business's success or failure. You may start your entrepreneurial path with clarity and confidence if you know what it takes to be an entrepreneur, what characteristics successful entrepreneurs possess, and the advantages and difficulties involved.

Chapter Seven

Building Your Brand

The process of giving your company a distinctive character that sets it apart from rivals and appeals to your target market is known as branding. A powerful brand may shape consumer perception, increase loyalty, and establish trust—all of which will eventually help your company succeed in the long run.

The following are the main justifications for the importance of branding: - **Recognition:** A powerful brand helps people remember and recognize your company.

Trust: Professional and consistent branding contributes to the development of consumers' reputation and trust.

Customer Loyalty: Emotional bonds may be cultivated between a brand and its ideals, encouraging repeat business.

Competitive Advantage: A strong brand distinguishes you from rivals and draws attention to your special selling features.

Business worth: A strong brand may raise the worth of your company and draw in new partners and investors.

Establishing a Personal Brand

Everything that represents your company, both visually and verbally, is part of your brand identity. It's the way you convey to your audience the essence, core principles, and promise of your brand.

How to build a powerful brand identity:

Define Your Brand's Purpose and Values: Clearly state the purpose, key values, and principles of your company. This is your brand's cornerstone.

Know Your Audience: To successfully customize your brand messaging, be aware of the demands, tastes, and behaviors of your target market.

Create a Unique Brand Name: Pick a name that captures the spirit of your company and is simple to recall.

Create a Logo: Create a logo that embodies your company's identity and is adaptable enough to be utilized across a range of media.

Select Brand Colours and Typography: Make sure your color scheme and font choices complement your brand's personality and elicit the feelings you want people to feel.

Create a Brand Voice and Tone: Identify the verbal communication style of your brand, including whether it is formal, approachable, lighthearted, or authoritative.

Create a slogan: Condense your brand's promise or main message into a short, memorable slogan.

Consistency is Key: Make sure all brand components are applied consistently throughout all touchpoints, including packaging, marketing materials, and your website and social media accounts.

Formulating a Marketing Plan

A marketing plan describes how you want to reach your target market and sell your brand. It entails determining the appropriate channels, establishing campaigns that complement your brand identity, and formulating marketing objectives.

How to create a marketing plan:

Set Specific Objectives: Identify the objectives you have for your marketing campaigns, such as expanding your audience, boosting sales, or raising brand awareness.

Know Your Audience: Obtain knowledge about the characteristics, passions, and problems of your target audience by conducting market research.

Select Your Marketing Channels: Determine which avenues—such as social media, email marketing, content marketing, or paid advertising—will help you reach your target audience the most successfully.

Create Engaging Content: Provide material that expresses your brand identity and connects with your audience. Posts on social media, videos, infographics, and blogs may all fall under this category.

Create a material Calendar: Arrange and plan your material so that you can communicate with your audience regularly and on time.

Measure and Analyse: Use analytics tools to monitor the effectiveness of your marketing campaigns. Analyze your approach and make data-driven changes based on what's working.

Making Use of Social Media

Social media is an effective tool for brand development and promotion. It enables you to interact with your audience, tell the story of your company, and increase customer traffic.

Select the Correct Platforms: Pick social media sites where your target market is most engaged and that complement your brand.

Create a Consistent Profile: Make sure that your bio, cover photo, and profile photographs are all in line with your brand identity on every site.

Involve Your Audience: Return the favor by addressing messages, comments, and mentions to establish rapport and promote a feeling of community.

Share Valuable information: To keep your audience interested, provide educational, entertaining, or motivational information.

Use Visuals: Make your material more visually attractive and shareable by utilizing graphics, videos, and photographs.

Make Use of Hashtags: Utilise pertinent hashtags to expand your posts' exposure and viewership.

Monitor and Adjust: Review your social media statistics frequently to determine what kinds of material appeal to your audience and modify your approach appropriately.

You can create a memorable brand, stick out in the market, and engage your audience more deeply by establishing a strong brand identity, creating an efficient marketing plan, and using social media.

Chapter Eight

Getting Past Obstacles

An entrepreneur must overcome several obstacles in launching and operating a firm. Recognizing these difficulties will enable you to anticipate and get ready for them.

Financial Management: It can be challenging to sustain profitability, secure finance, and manage cash flow, particularly in the early phases of your company.

Time Management: For new business owners, setting priorities and juggling a variety of obligations may be extremely difficult.

Market Competition: It takes constant work and creativity to stand out in a competitive market and keep ahead of the competition.

Customer Acquisition and Retention: While difficult and expensive, bringing in new business and keeping hold of current clientele are essential for expansion.

Regulatory Compliance: Adhering to industry and regulatory rules may be difficult and time-consuming.

Scaling Operations: As your company expands, it may be difficult to handle higher demand, hire more staff, and scale operations effectively.

Technological Changes: Adapting to new tools and keeping up with technological improvements can be challenging, but doing so is essential to being competitive.

Economic Uncertainty: Outside variables that affect your firm include market swings, worldwide happenings, and economic downturns.

Techniques for Solving Problems

Overcoming obstacles and assuring the success of your company depend on your ability to solve problems effectively. The following techniques can assist you in solving difficulties successfully:

- **Identify the Issue:** Clearly state the issue that you are dealing with. Compile data, assess the circumstances, and identify the underlying reason.

- **Generate Solutions:** Make a list of potential remedies and long-term plans while brainstorming ideas. Seek feedback from your group to acquire a variety of viewpoints.

- **Evaluate Options:** Weigh the benefits and drawbacks of each option, taking into account aspects including cost, impact potential, and practicality.

- **Make a Decision:** Based on your assessment, select the best course of action. Decide with confidence and decisiveness.

- **Implement the Solution:** Create a strategy outlining the precise actions, who is responsible for what, and when to implement the solution that has been selected.

- **Monitor Progress:** Keep tabs on the development of your solution and tweak as necessary. Make sure the issue is being handled by periodically reviewing the circumstances.

- **Learn and Reflect:** Consider the experience once the issue has been resolved. Determine what was successful and what may be improved for resolving issues in the future.

Acquiring Knowledge from Setbacks

While it's an unavoidable aspect of being an entrepreneur, failure may also teach you important lessons. You may increase your chances of success in the future and develop as a business owner by accepting failure and learning from it.

1. Change Your Mindset: See failure not as a setback but as a chance to grow. Embrace a growth attitude that emphasizes ongoing development.

2. Analyse the Failure: Examine closely the issues that occurred. Determine the causes of the failure and recognize the lessons that may be used.

3. Seek Feedback: To get other viewpoints on the setback and pinpoint areas in need of development, get input from your mentors, customers, and team.

4. Adapt and Pivot: Make the required adjustments to your company's procedures, product offers, and business strategy by drawing on the lessons learned from failure. Be adaptable and open to trying other strategies.

5. Share Your Experience: Tell people about your mistake and the lessons you took away from it. This might support the development of an open and learning-oriented culture inside your company.

6. Remain Resilient: Keep your will and fortitude intact. Recall that perseverance is essential for long-term success and that failure is only a temporary setback.

7. Celebrate Small Wins: Along the road, acknowledge and commemorate your little victories. This might give you a positive attitude and inspire you to keep going.

Through the use of effective problem-solving techniques, anticipation of typical business issues, and learning from mistakes, you can traverse the ups and downs of entrepreneurship with resilience and confidence.

Chapter Nine

Staying Ahead of Industry Trends

Keeping up with market developments is crucial to preserving your competitive advantage and making sure your company stays relevant. The following tactics will assist you in remaining informed:

Subscribe to sector Publications: Read periodicals, magazines, and web publications about your sector regularly. These resources frequently offer insightful information on new developments in technology, trends, and market dynamics.

Join Professional Associations: Join groups and associations within your sector. These organizations provide information, chances for networking, and updates on recent advancements in the field.

Attend Conferences and Trade Shows: Take part in business gatherings to discover fresh goods, services, and breakthroughs. Additionally, networking opportunities with peers and industry leaders are offered by these gatherings.

Follow Thinking Leaders: Monitor significant individuals and thinking leaders within your field. To learn about their opinions and forecasts, keep up with their publications, blogs, and social media pages.

Participate in Online Communities: Join discussion boards, forums, and social media groups where experts in your field exchange knowledge, trends, and firsthand accounts.

Observe Rivals: Keep tabs on what your rivals are up to. Examine their tactics, offerings, and promotional activities to find patterns and business prospects.

Creating and Modifying

Adaptability and innovation are essential for long-term corporate success and growth. Here are some strategies for encouraging creativity and flexibility in your company:

Promote an Innovative Culture: Establish a setting that values and promotes creativity and innovation. Encourage open dialogue and provide staff members with chances to contribute their views.

Invest in Research and Development: Provide funds for the investigation of novel goods, services, and technological advancements through research and development (R&D). Continue to be inquisitive and proactive in your search for novel and creative solutions.

Test and Improve: Don't be scared to try out novel concepts. Before putting them into practice entirely, test them in a limited setting, as get input, and make any necessary changes.

Embrace Change: Show flexibility by being prepared to modify your company's procedures, tactics, and business model as circumstances demand. In a market that is always changing, adaptability is essential for staying relevant.

Use Technology: Keep up with technology developments and integrate pertinent technologies into your company's daily operations. This may spur innovation, increase productivity, and improve consumer experiences.

Collaborate and Network: Join forces with startups, other companies, and industry leaders to exchange resources, ideas, and expertise. Working together can result in fresh perspectives and possibilities.

Maintaining your competitive edge in your field and developing as a corporate leader requires ongoing education and professional growth. Here's how to make continual learning your top priority:

Enrol in Workshops and Courses: Expand your knowledge and abilities by taking advantage of online workshops, seminars, and courses. Seek for courses that are pertinent to the demands of your company and sector.

Acquire certificates: Get professional certificates that can enhance your reputation and give you an in-depth understanding of particular fields.

Read Books and Articles: Consistently read business, leadership, and industry-related books, articles, and whitepapers. Reading regularly keeps you informed and motivated.

Attend Webinars and Podcasts: Take part in webinars and tune in to podcasts led by professionals in the field. These formats provide practical methods to study while lounging around your house or place of business.

Seek Mentorship: Look for mentors who, from their experience, can offer advice, encouragement, and insightful advice. You may advance both professionally and personally with mentoring.

Take Part in Networking Events: To meet other professionals and get insight from their experiences, go to networking events, both in person and virtually. Networking may lead to new partnerships and possibilities.

Promote Team Development: Invest in your team members' career advancement. Provide workshops, training courses, and chances for skill development. An informed and competent staff adds to your company's overall success.

You can make sure your company stays ahead of the curve and continues to flourish in a dynamic market by being up-to-date with industry trends, encouraging innovation, and placing a high priority on continuing education and professional development.

Chapter Ten

Case Studies and Success Stories

Motivational Business Adventures

Gaining knowledge and inspiration from other businesses' triumphs and setbacks may be quite beneficial. Here are some motivational tales of entrepreneurial success to draw lessons from:

Spanx - Sara Blakely - Travelling: With $5,000 in savings and a creative idea for footless pantyhose, Sara Blakely founded Spanx. She had no experience in fashion or business, but she was determined to follow her dream.

- **Difficulties:** She battled to get her product into shops and was met with a lot of manufacturer rejections.

- **Result:** Spanx is now a well-known brand worldwide, and Blakely became the country's youngest self-made female millionaire. Her experience serves as a reminder of the value of tenacity, creativity, and confidence in your offering.

Elon Musk - SpaceX and Tesla - Travel: Elon Musk is well-known for his audacious attempts to explore space and develop electric cars. He became the CEO of Tesla Motors and established SpaceX after making his fortune with PayPal.

- **Difficulties:** Both businesses had to deal with serious technological obstacles, financial setbacks, and public and industry mistrust.

- **Result:** Tesla transformed the market for electric vehicles, and SpaceX made significant advancements in space exploration, such as the use of reusable rockets. Musk's path demonstrates the importance of having a big-picture mindset, perseverance, and constant invention.

Howard Schultz - Starbucks: Starbucks was a little vendor of coffee beans before Howard Schultz built it into a massive chain of coffee shops. After joining the firm in the early 1980s, he had the idea to create a "third place" where individuals could unwind and socialize between work and home.

- **Difficulties:** When trying to grow the business, Schultz fell into opposition from the original proprietors as well as financial challenges.

- **Result:** Starbucks is a household name in high-end coffee culture and has hundreds of outlets globally. The tale of Schultz exemplifies the value of brand development, customer experience, and vision.

Oprah Winfrey - OWN (Oprah Winfrey Network): From a difficult upbringing, Oprah Winfrey went on to succeed as a media magnate and philanthropist. She started her own production business and then owned her cable network.

- **Difficulties:** Racial and gender prejudice, as well as the early difficulties of starting a new network, were among the major challenges Winfrey had to overcome.

- **Result:** She established a media empire and rose to prominence as one of the world's most powerful women. Through her path, Winfrey has demonstrated the value of being genuine, persevering, and using one's platform to make a positive difference.

Takeaways from Profitable Enterprises

Aspiring entrepreneurs may learn a lot from examining the tactics and methods of profitable companies:

Apple Inc. - Innovation and Design: Apple has distinguished itself in the technology sector with its dedication to innovation and elegant design. Concentrate on developing products that provide outstanding user experiences.

Brand Loyalty: By producing high-quality goods and maintaining a consistent brand, Apple has amassed a devoted following of customers. Put the needs of your customers and brand consistency first.

Amazon - Client-First Strategy: Amazon's unwavering commitment to providing excellent customer service—from tailored suggestions to effective delivery services—is the key to its success. Customers' wants and convenience should always come first.

Integration: Amazon began as an online book retailer before diversifying into other industries, such as streaming and cloud computing. Be willing to change up your product line in response to market demands.

Nike - Storytelling and Marketing: Nike's emotive narrative and potent marketing strategies connect with their audience on an emotional level. Craft a captivating brand story that speaks to the goals and values of your target audience.

Partnerships and Endorsements: Nike's brand recognition has increased dramatically as a result of its partnerships with athletes and influencers. Make use of smart alliances to expand the visibility and credibility of your brand.

Airbnb - Disruptive Innovation: By allowing individuals to rent out their homes, Airbnb transformed the hospitality sector. Seek for chances to use creative ideas to upend established markets.

Building Community: Through the development of a robust community among hosts and guests, Airbnb promoted loyalty and trust. Concentrate on creating a brand-supporting community.

Fifth, Google - Workplace Culture: Google's emphasis on a creative and upbeat work environment has drawn top talent and contributed to its success. Invest to provide your staff with a creative and encouraging work atmosphere.

Decisions Driven by Data: Google employs data analytics to better its products and guide its strategy. Make judgments based on data, and use data to streamline company processes.

Gaining knowledge from these remarkable journeys and prosperous enterprises will help you overcome obstacles, develop successful strategies, and steer your firm in the direction of success.

Conclusion

Recap and Final Thoughts

Starting a business is an exciting and challenging journey that requires careful planning, resilience, and continuous learning. Throughout this book, we have covered the essential steps and strategies to help you build a successful business from the ground up. Here's a quick recap of what we've discussed:

Understanding Entrepreneurship: We explored what entrepreneurship is, the traits of successful entrepreneurs, and the benefits and challenges of starting a business.

Planning Your Business: We delved into developing your business idea, conducting market research, creating a business plan, and choosing the right business structure.

Funding Your Business: We looked at various funding options, from bootstrapping and loans to venture capital and crowdfunding.

Setting Up Your Business: We discussed the legal aspects of starting a business, including registering your business, obtaining licenses and permits, and setting up your accounting system.

Building Your Brand: We emphasized the importance of branding, creating a brand identity, developing a marketing strategy, and utilizing social media.

Growing Your Business: We covered strategies for scaling your business, hiring and managing a team, and optimizing operations.

Overcoming Challenges: We addressed common business challenges, problem-solving strategies, and learning from failure.

Staying Ahead: We highlighted the importance of keeping up with industry trends, innovating and adapting, and continuing education and professional development.

Success Stories and Case Studies: We shared inspirational entrepreneurial journeys and lessons learned from successful businesses.

Encouragement for Aspiring Entrepreneurs

Embarking on the entrepreneurial path is both rewarding and demanding. As you set out to start and grow your business, remember these key points:

Believe in Yourself: Confidence in your vision and abilities is crucial. Trust yourself and your potential to make your business a success.

Stay Resilient: Challenges and setbacks are inevitable. Use them as learning experiences and remain persistent in pursuing your goals.

Be Open to Learning: The business landscape is constantly evolving. Stay curious, seek new knowledge, and adapt to changes.

Build a Support Network: Surround yourself with mentors, peers, and a supportive team who can offer guidance, encouragement, and assistance.

Celebrate Small Wins: Recognize and celebrate your progress, no matter how small. Each step forward is a testament to your hard work and dedication.

Your entrepreneurial journey is uniquely yours, and the lessons you learn along the way will shape you and your business. Embrace the process, stay passionate, and never lose sight of your dreams.

Additional Resources

To further support your entrepreneurial journey, here are some additional resources that can provide valuable insights and guidance:

Books:
- **"The Lean Startup"** by **Eric Ries**
- **"Start with Why"** by **Simon Sinek**
- **"Good to Great"** by **Jim Collins**
- **"The E-Myth Revisited"** by **Michael E. Gerber**
- **"Zero to One"** by **Peter Thiel and Blake Masters**

Websites:
- [Entrepreneur](https://www.entrepreneur.com/)
- [Small Business Administration (SBA)](https://www.sba.gov/)
- [Inc.](https://www.inc.com/)
- [Harvard Business Review](https://hbr.org/)

Online Courses:
- Coursera ([Business Courses](https://www.coursera.org/browse/business))
- Udemy ([Entrepreneurship Courses](https://www.udemy.com/topic/entrepreneurship/))
- LinkedIn Learning ([Business Courses](https://www.linkedin.com/learning/topics/business))

Podcasts:
- **"How I Built This"** by **Guy Raz**
- **"The Tim Ferriss Show"** by **Tim Ferriss**
- **"Smart Passive Income"** by **Pat Flynn**
- **"Entrepreneurs on Fire"** by **John Lee Dumas**
- **"The GaryVee Audio Experience"** by **Gary Vaynerchuk**

These resources offer a wealth of information and inspiration to help you navigate the complexities of entrepreneurship. Remember, the journey of building a business is a continuous learning process, and these tools can provide the support and knowledge you need to succeed.

Thank you for embarking on this journey with us. We wish you all the best in your entrepreneurial endeavors and look forward to seeing the incredible impact you will make with your business.

www.ingramcontent.com/pod-product-compliance
Lightning Source LLC
Chambersburg PA
CBHW082237220526
45479CB00005B/1264